How To Draw Realistic Skulls Volume 9

Simple Guide to Drawing Skulls

How to Draw Skulls

By : Gala Publication

Published By :

Gala Publication

© Copyright 2015 – Gala Publication

ISBN-13: **978-1522786078**
ISBN-10: **1522786074**

Table of Contents

CHIBI SKULL

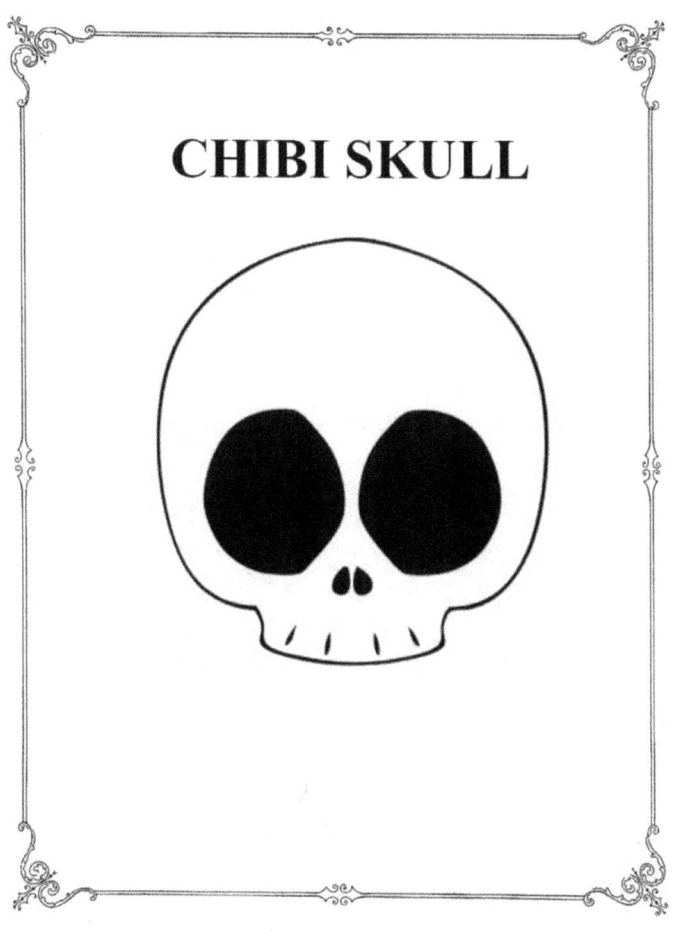

6

STEP 1

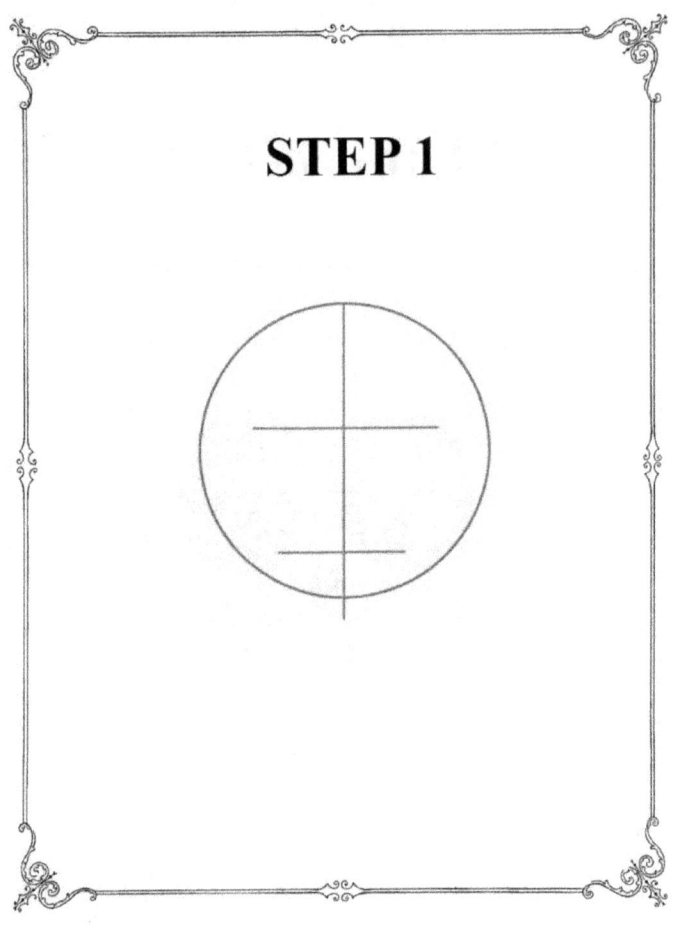

STEP 2

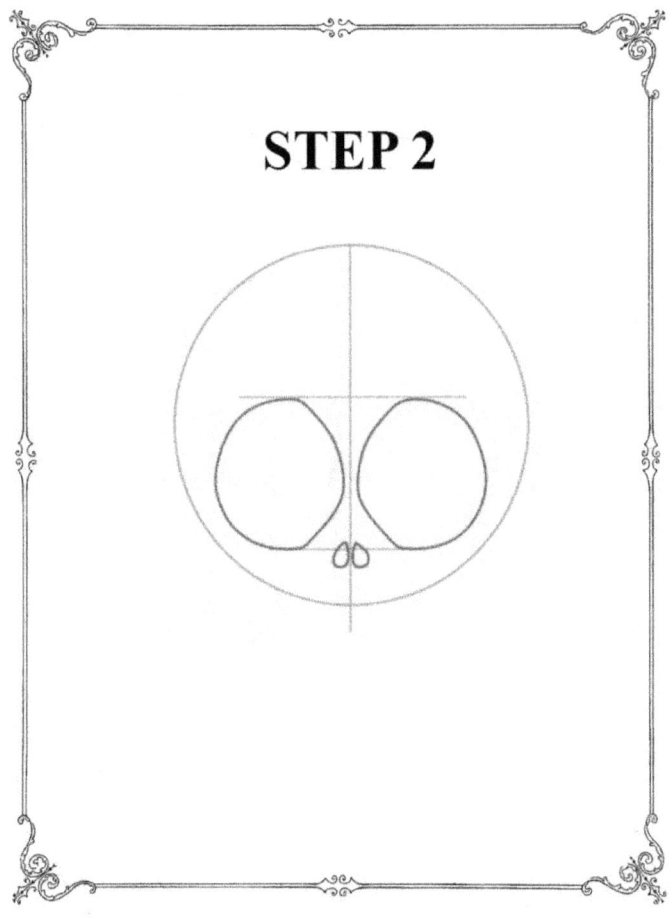

STEP 3

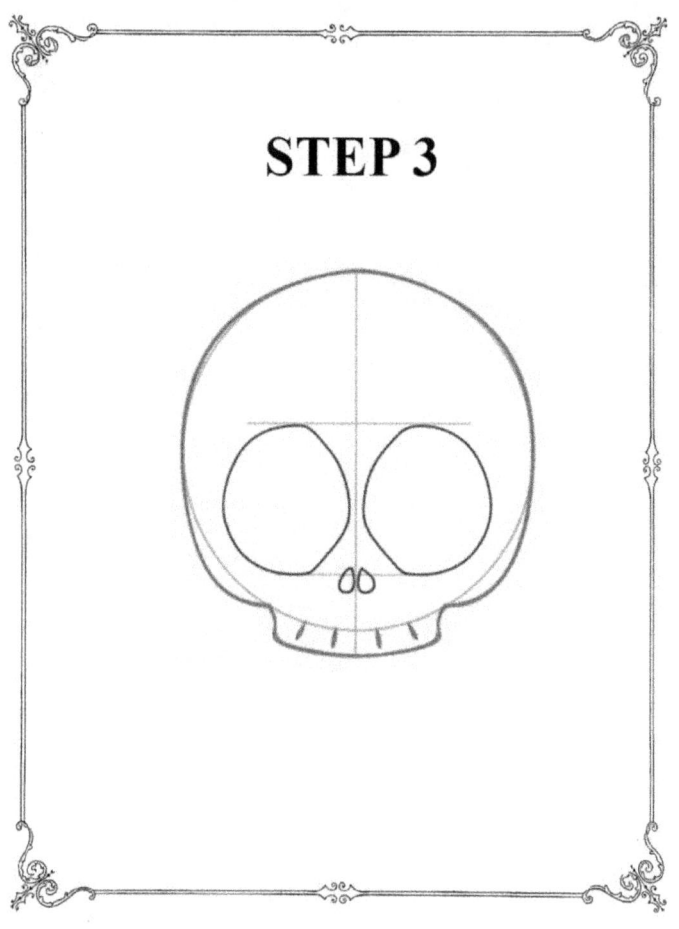

STEP 4

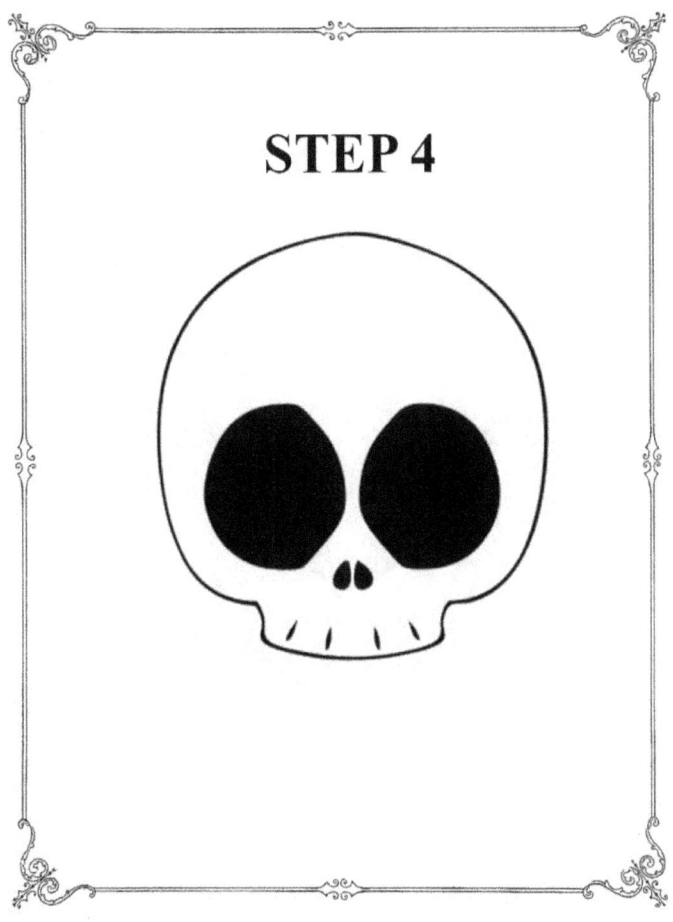

FIRE SKULL

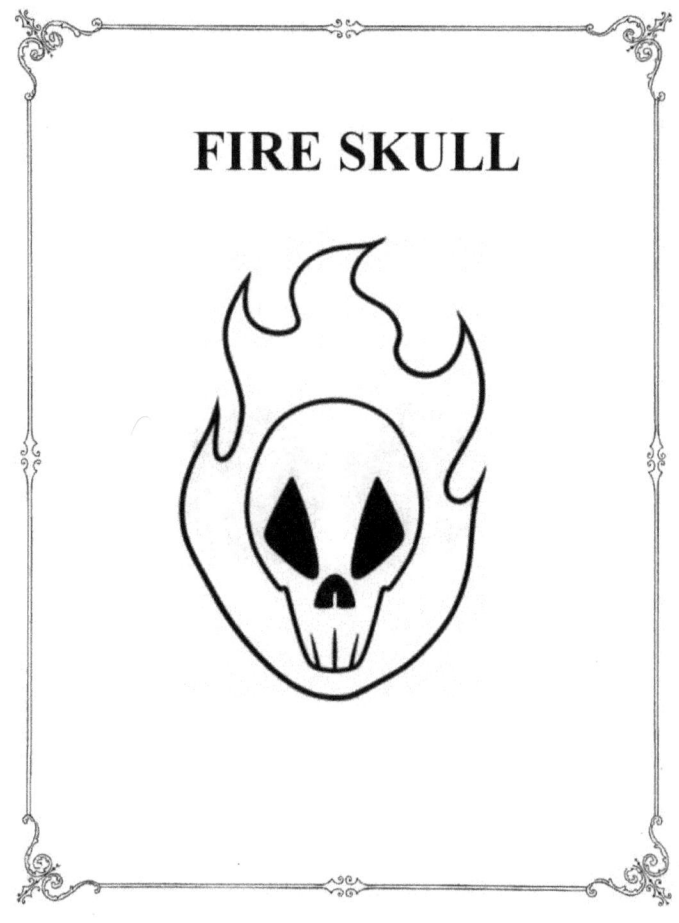

STEP 1

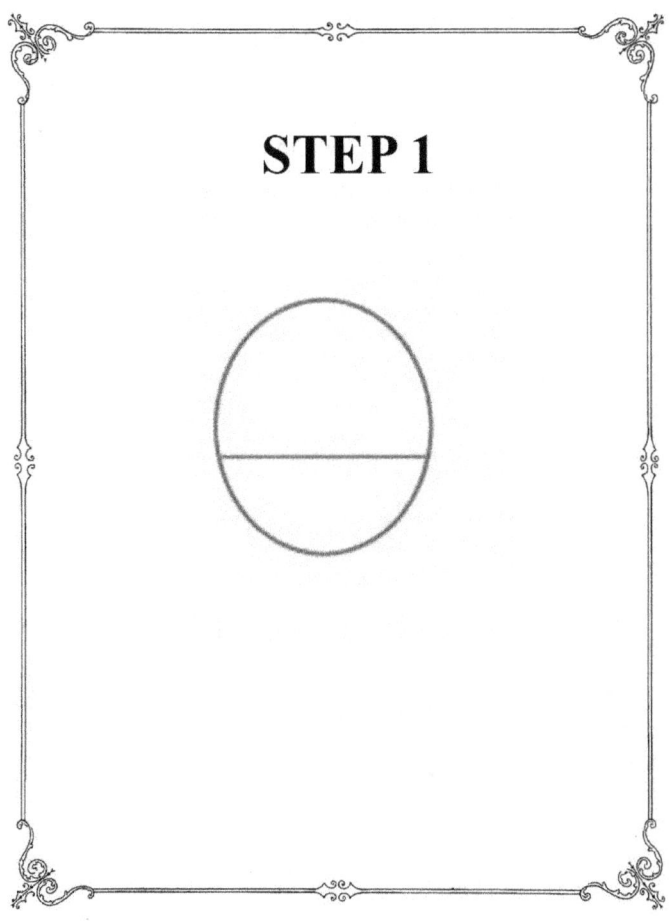

STEP 2

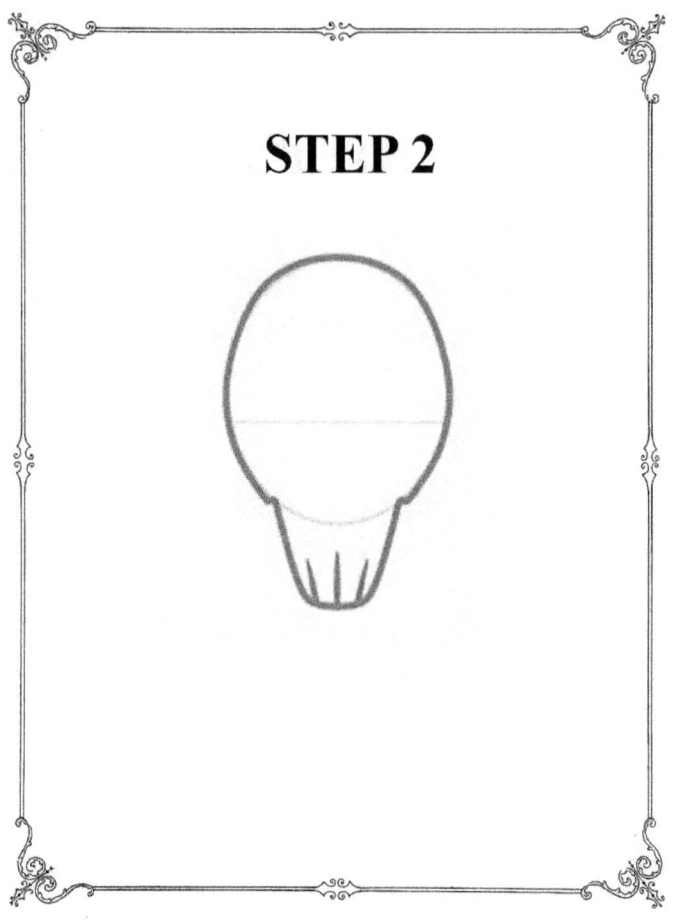

STEP 3

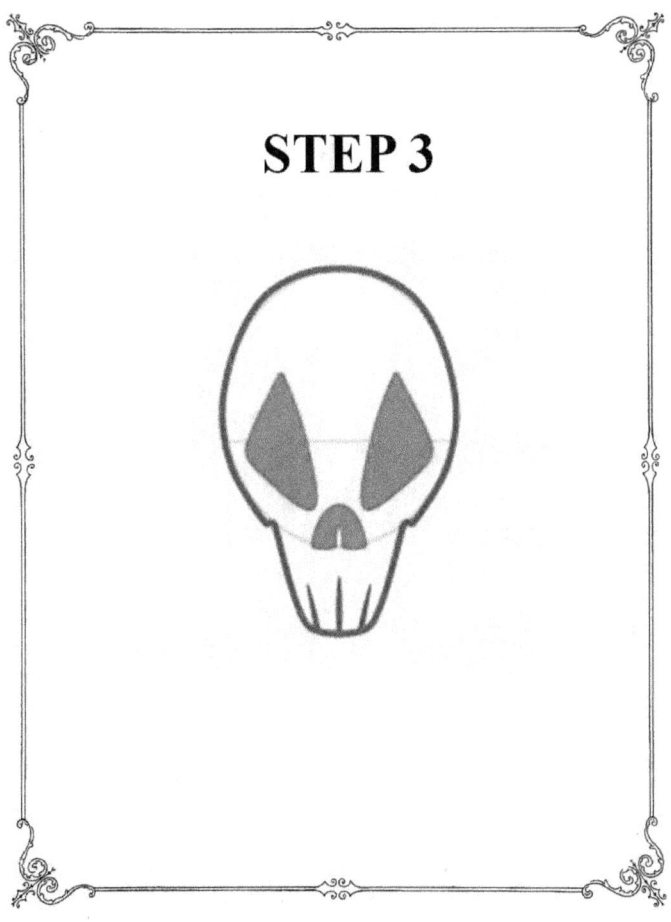

STEP 4

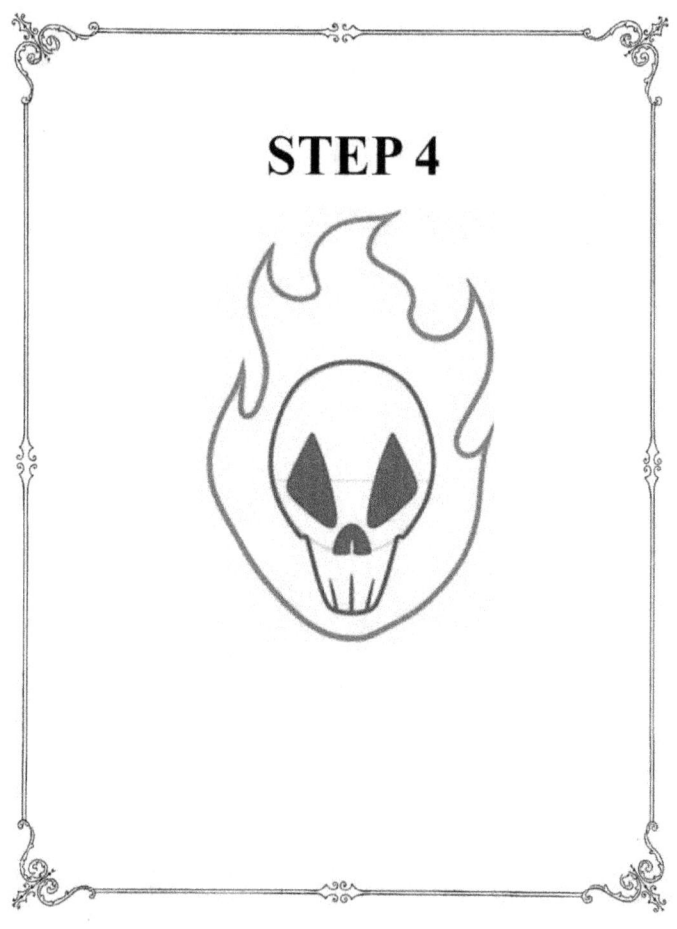

15

STEP 5

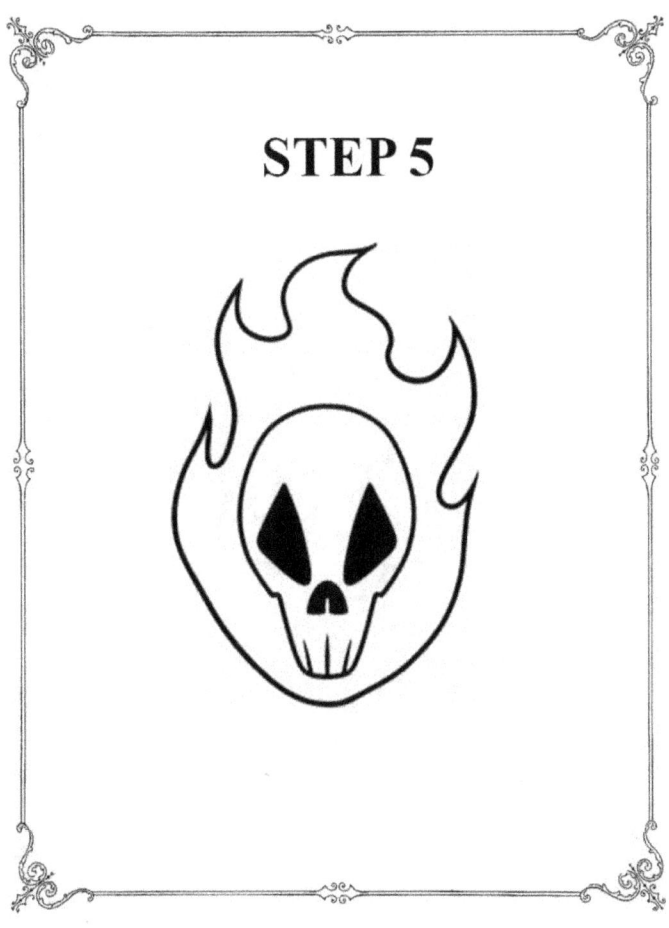

PIKACHU SKULL

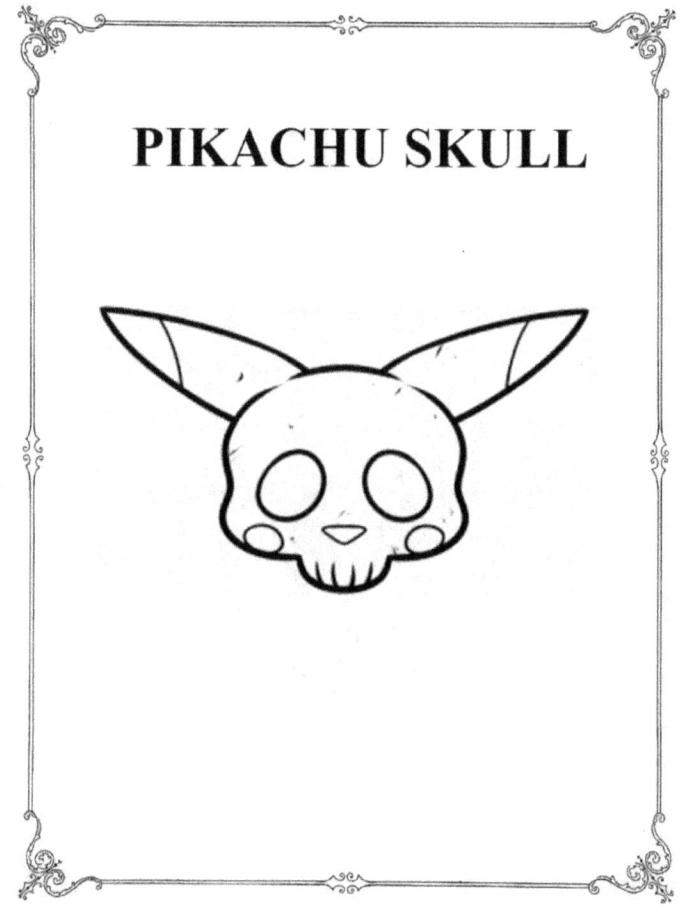

STEP 1

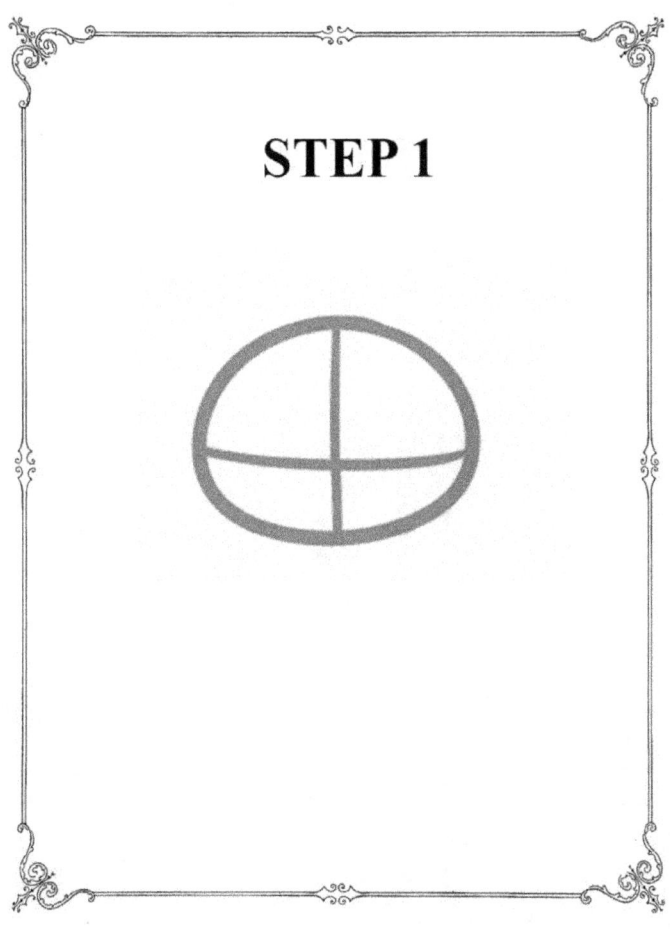

STEP 2

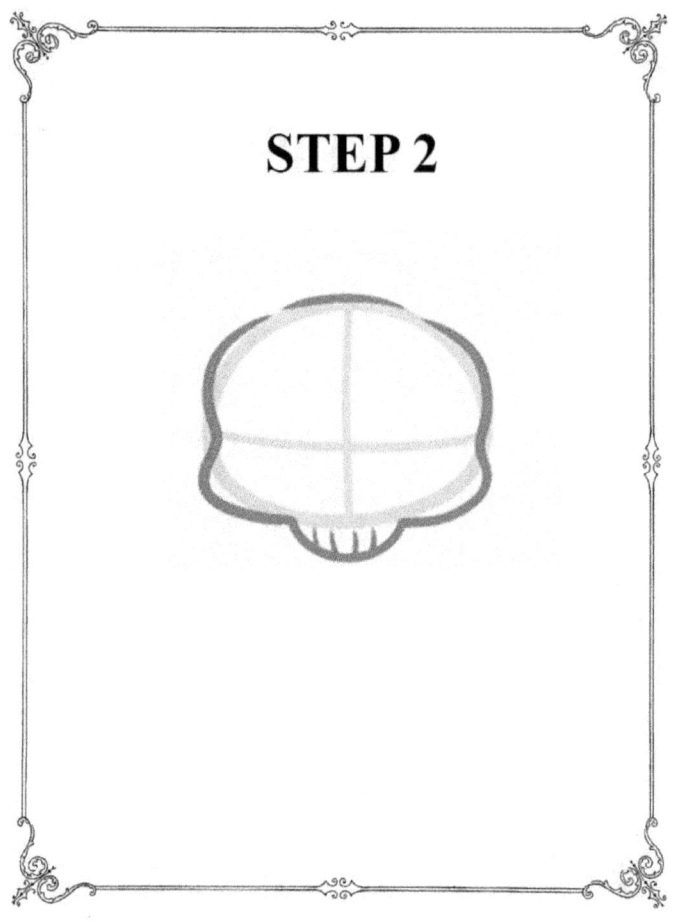

STEP 3

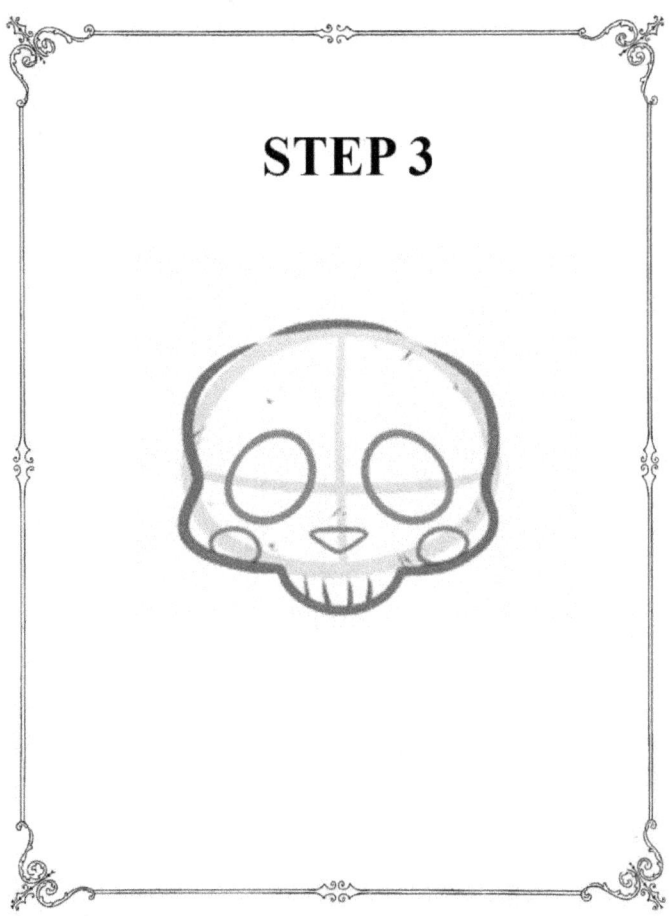

STEP 4

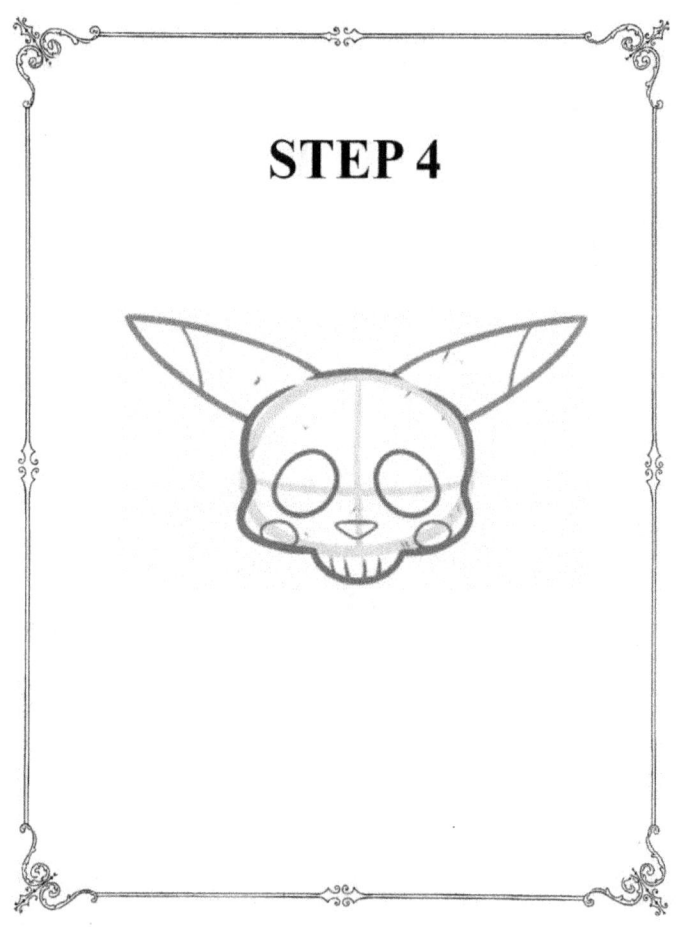

STEP 5

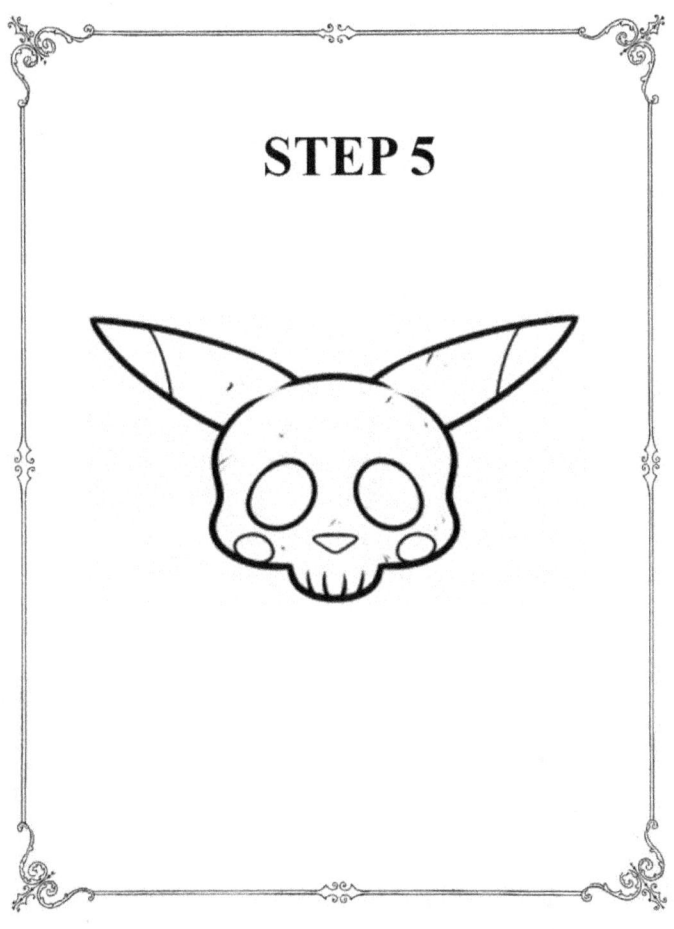

SHERIFF SKULL

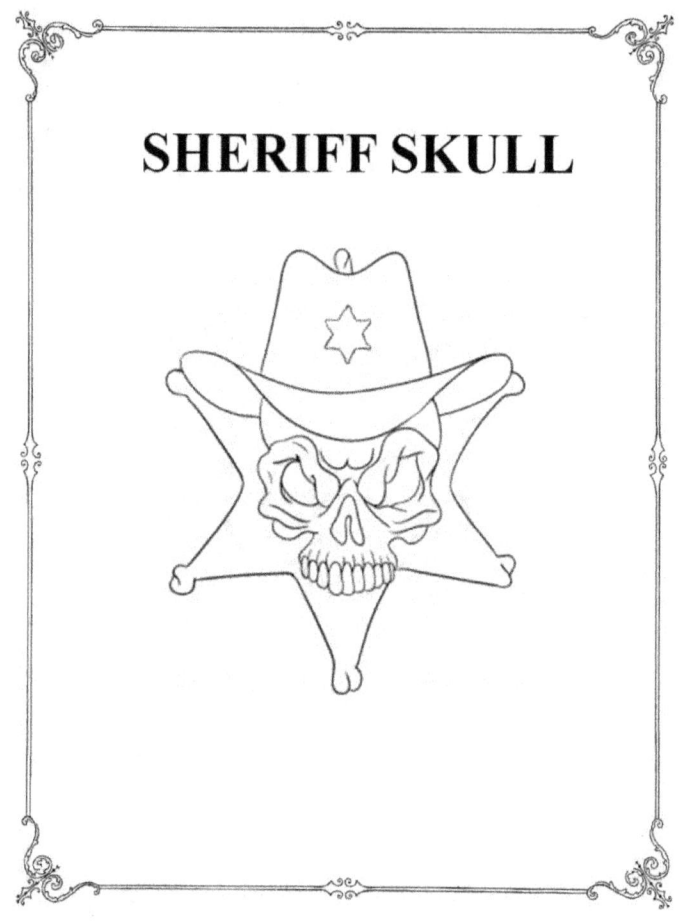

STEP 1

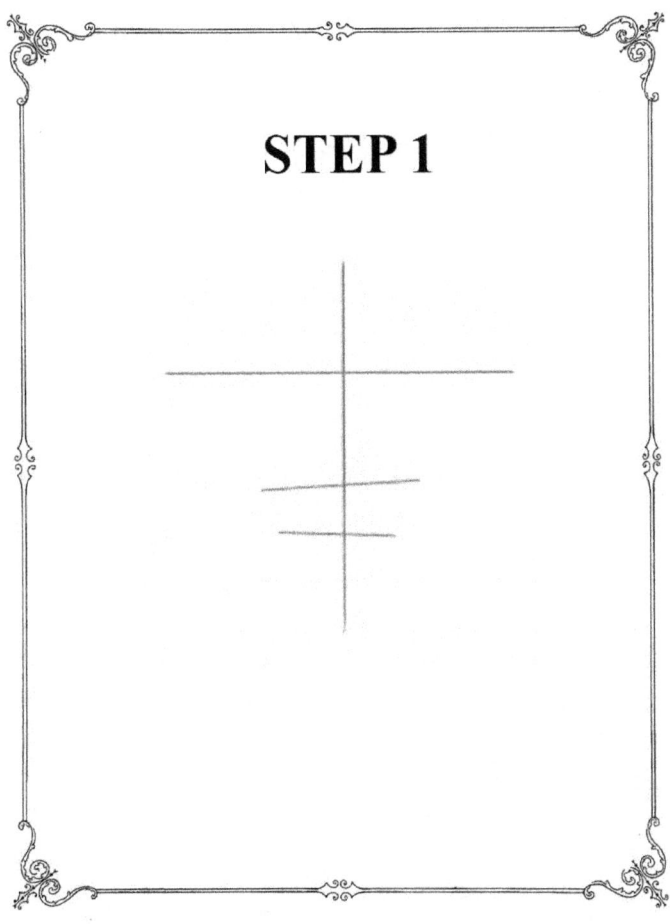

STEP 2

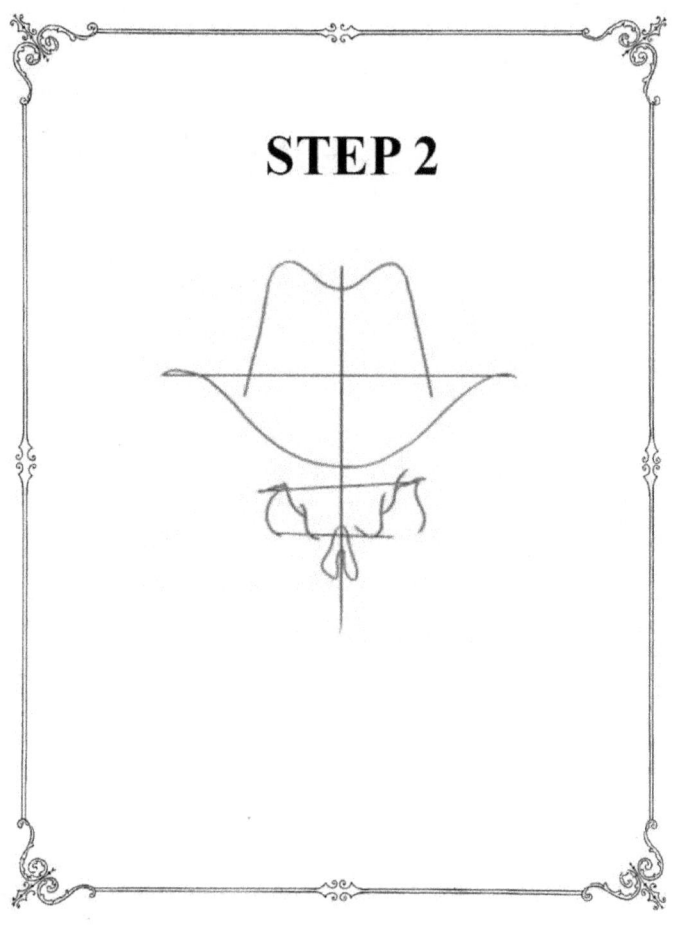

STEP 3

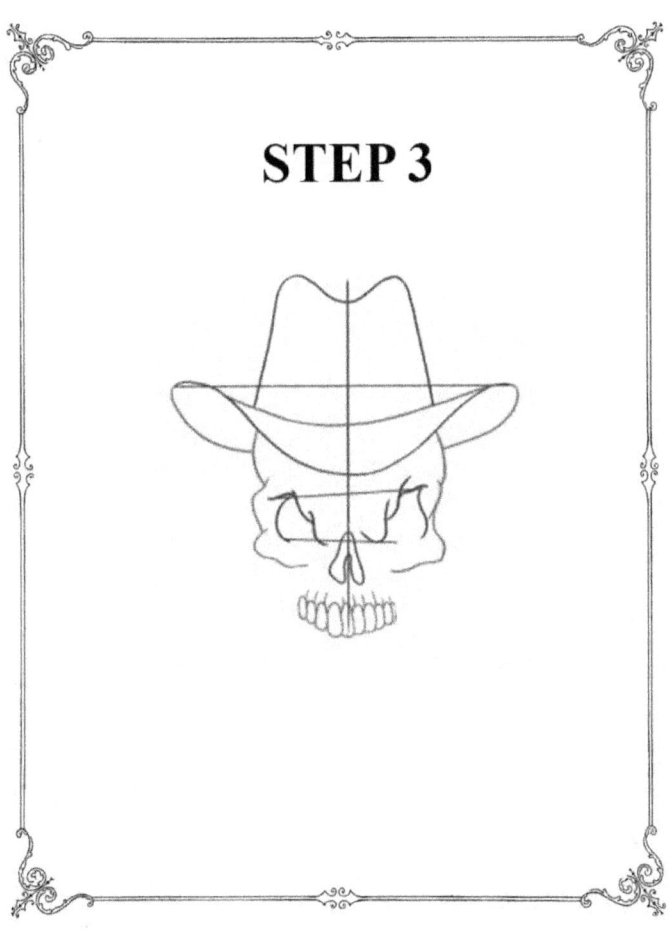

STEP 4

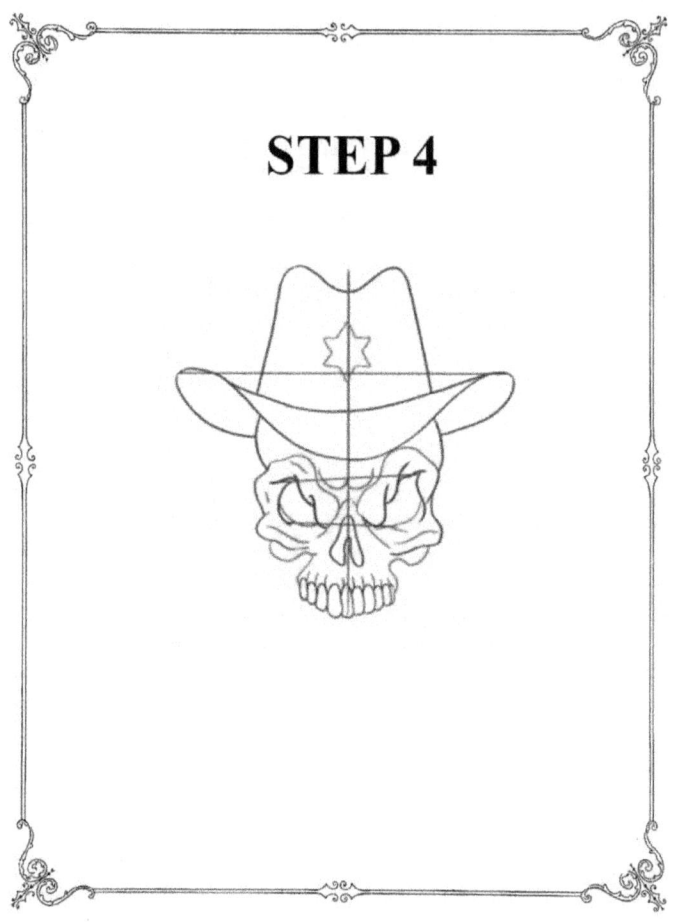

STEP 5

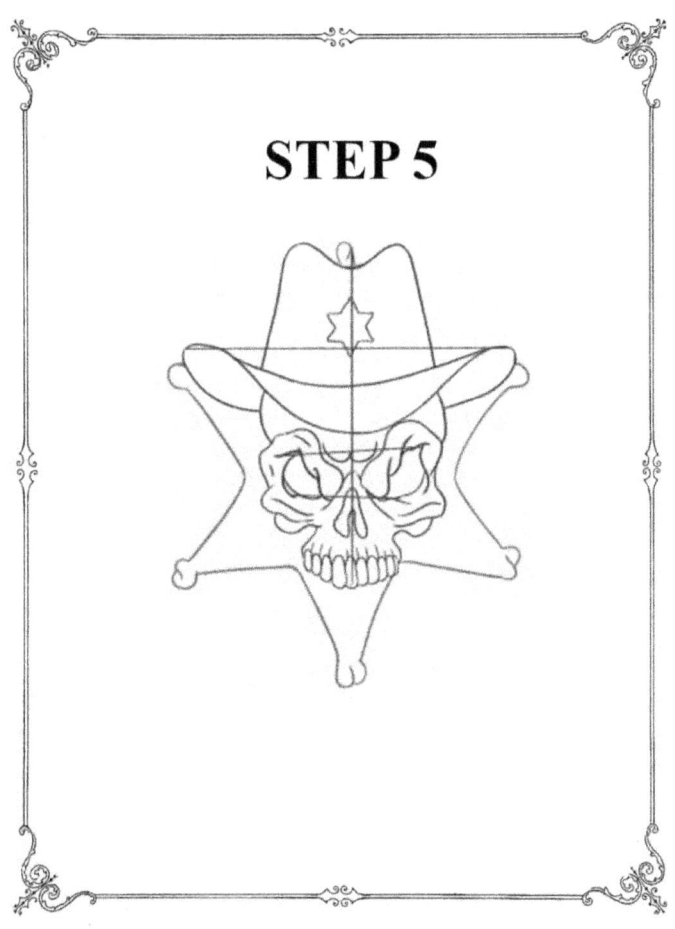

STEP 6

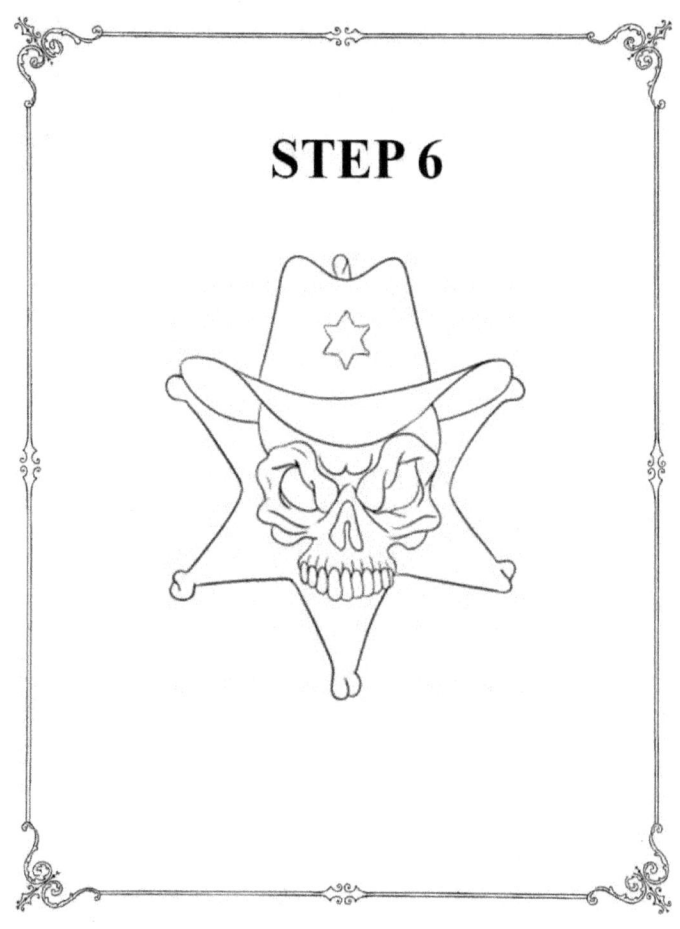

SNAKE SKULL

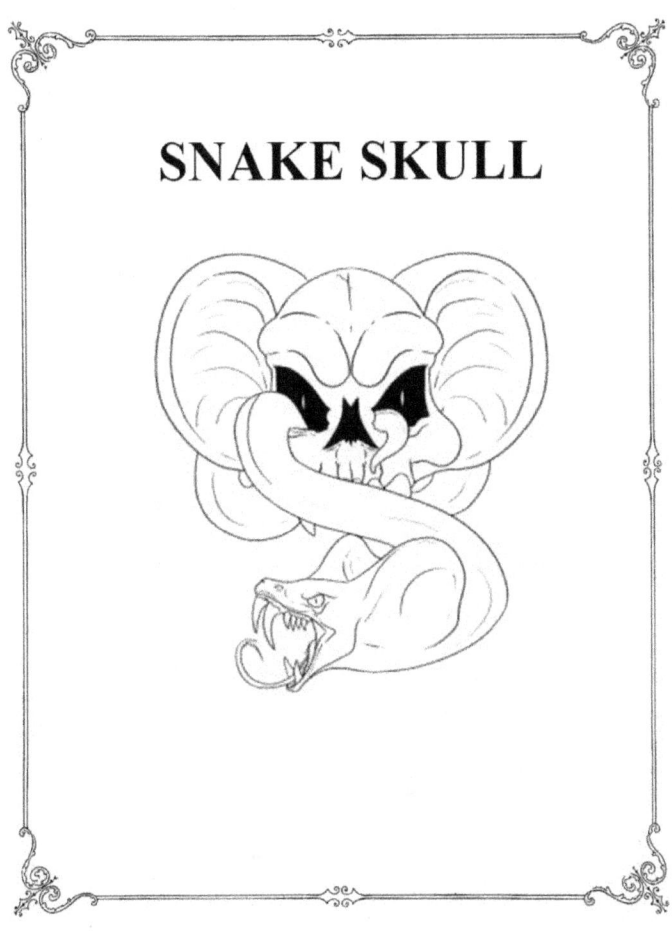

STEP 1

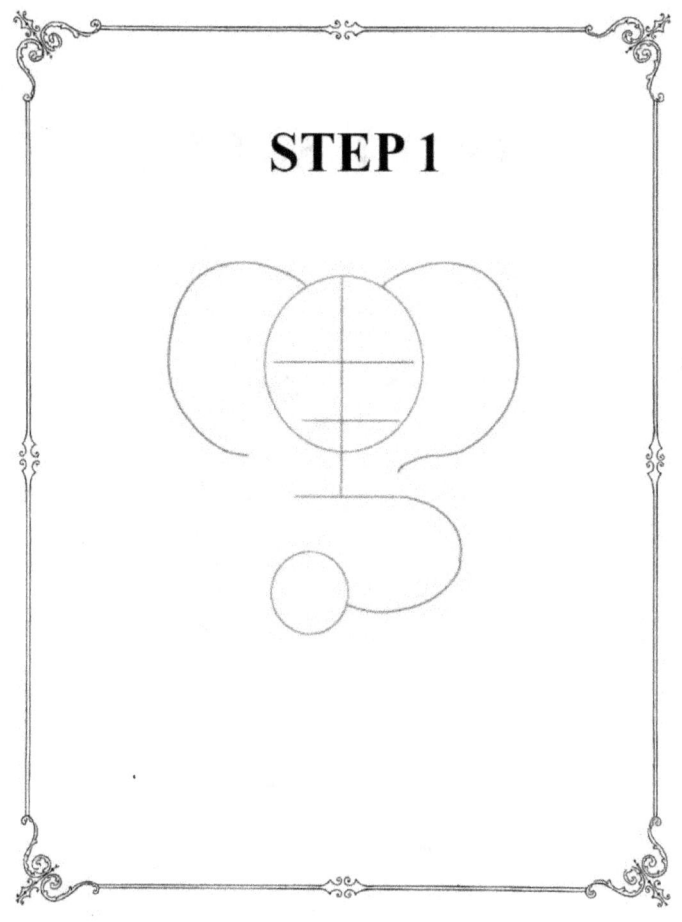

STEP 2

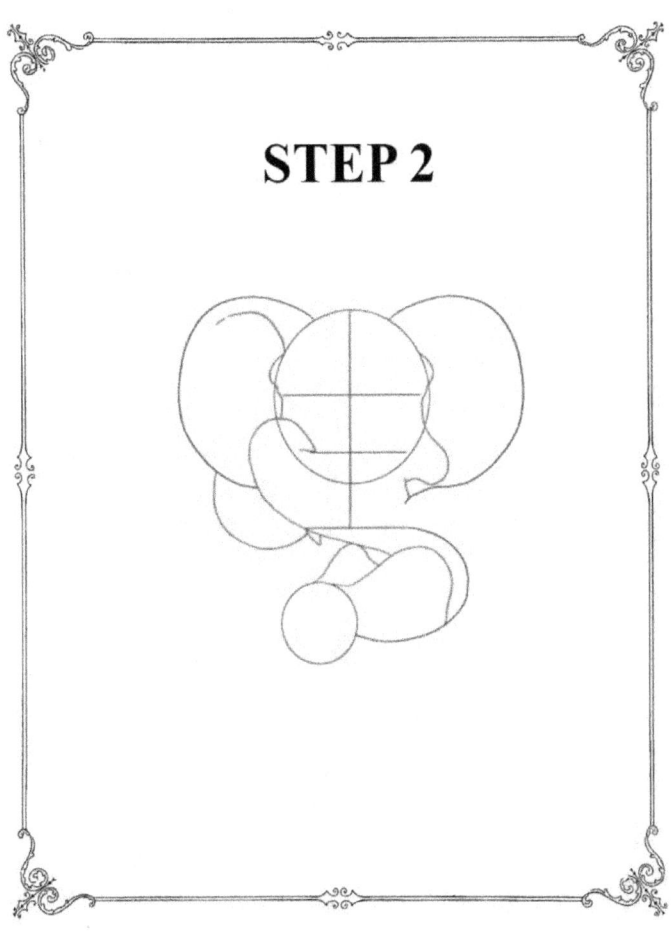

STEP 3

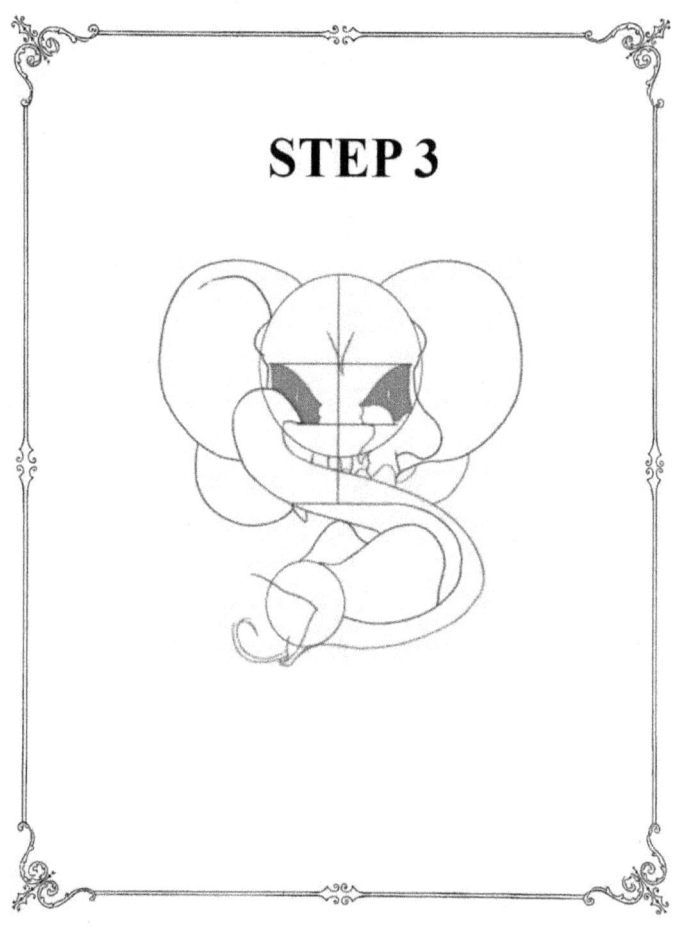

STEP 4

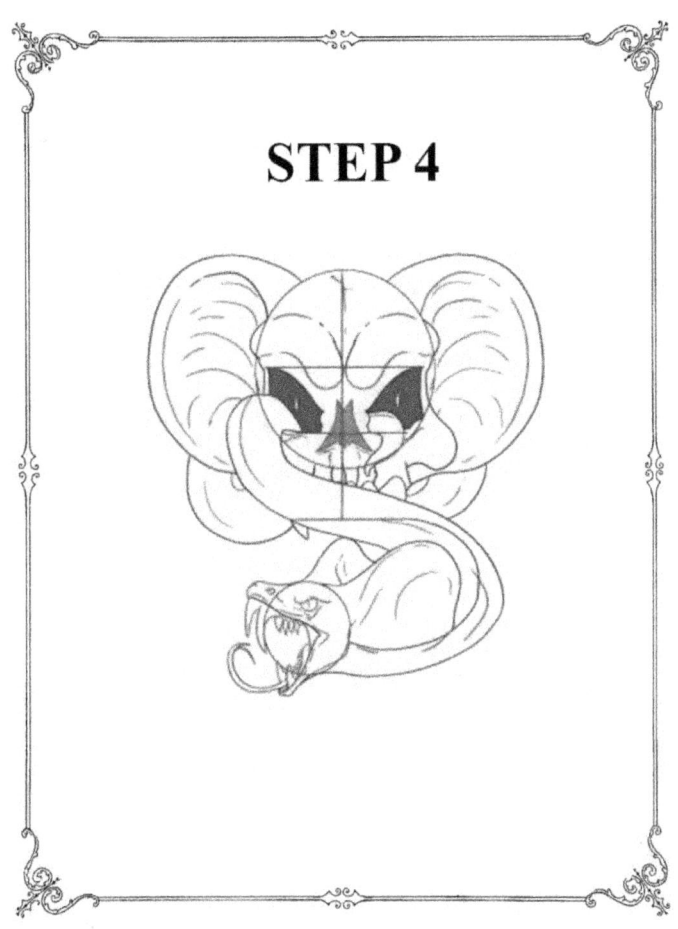

STEP 5

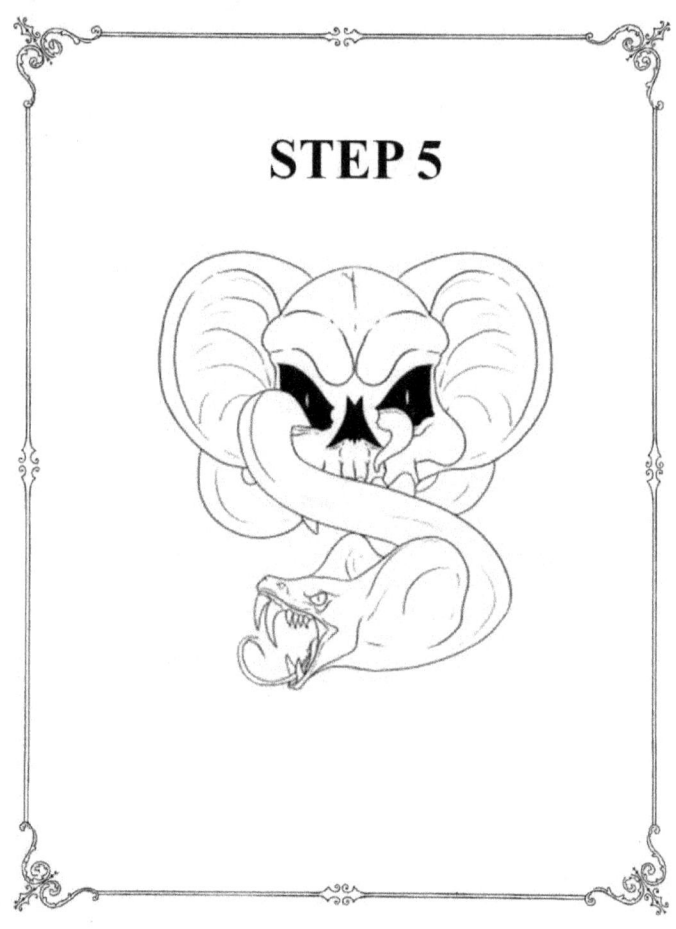

SOLDIER SKULL

STEP 1

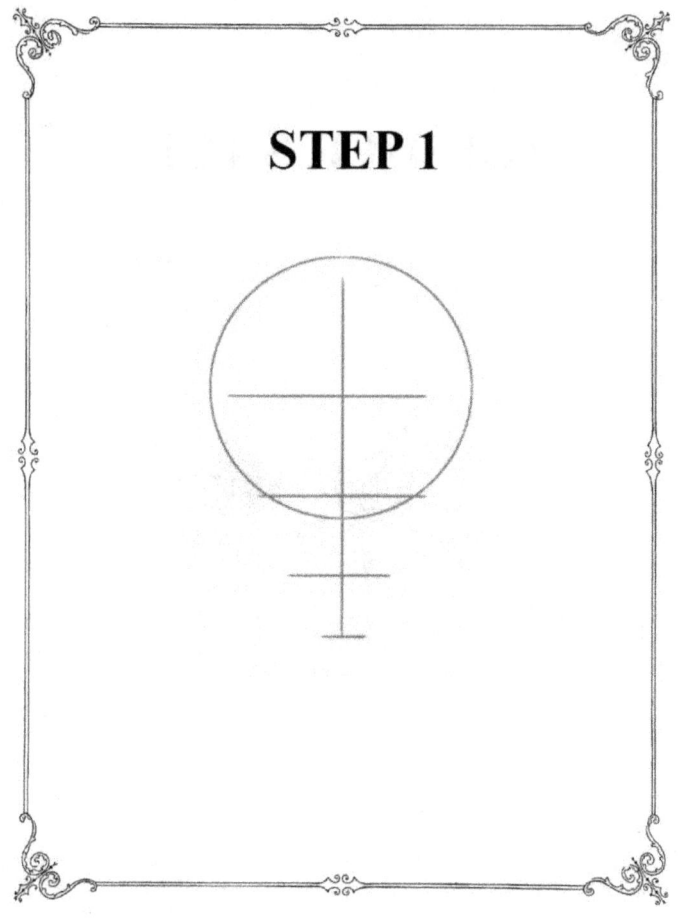

STEP 2

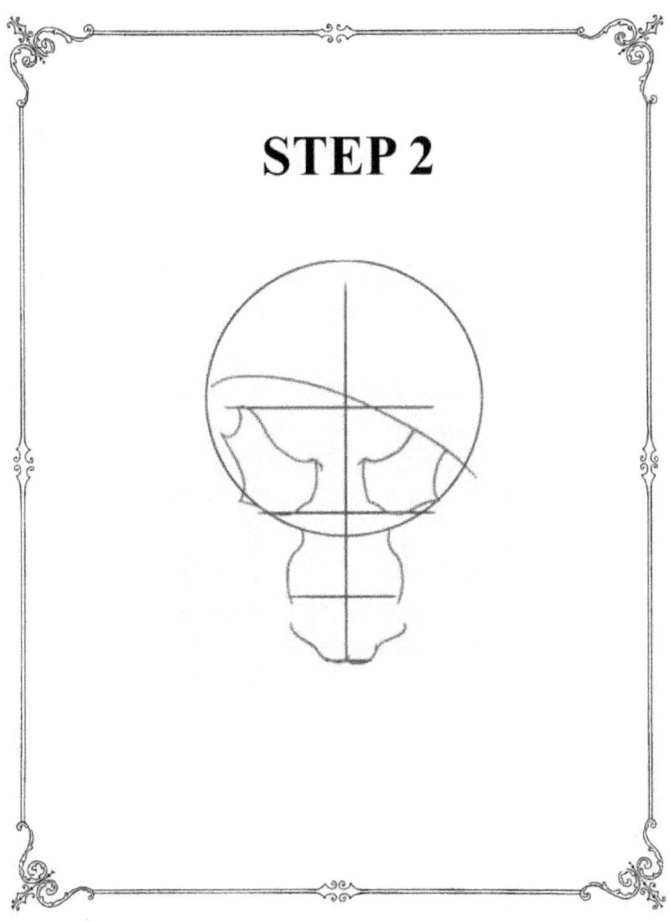

STEP 3

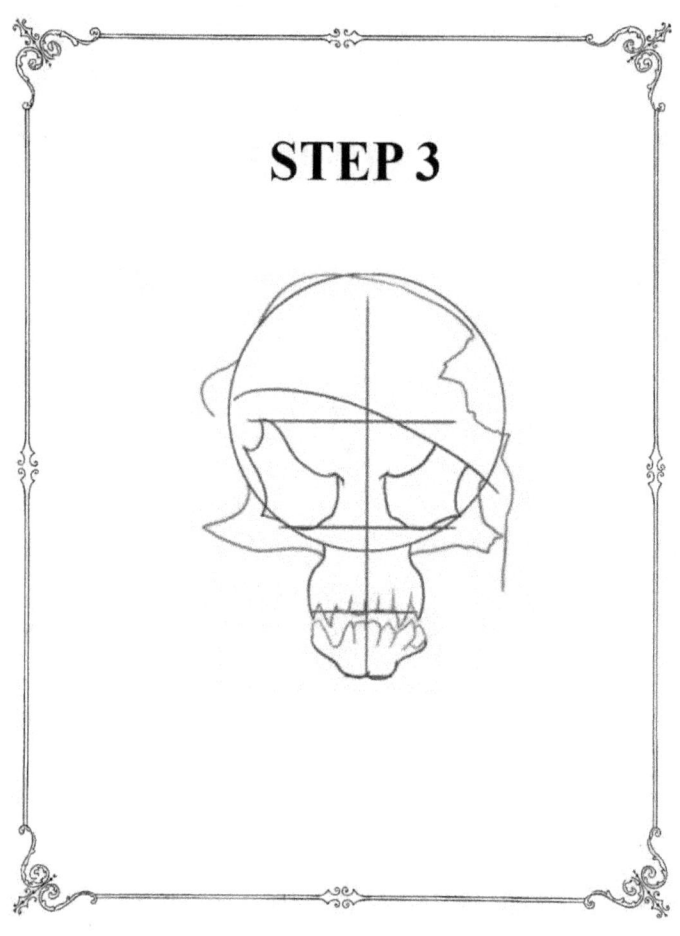

STEP 4

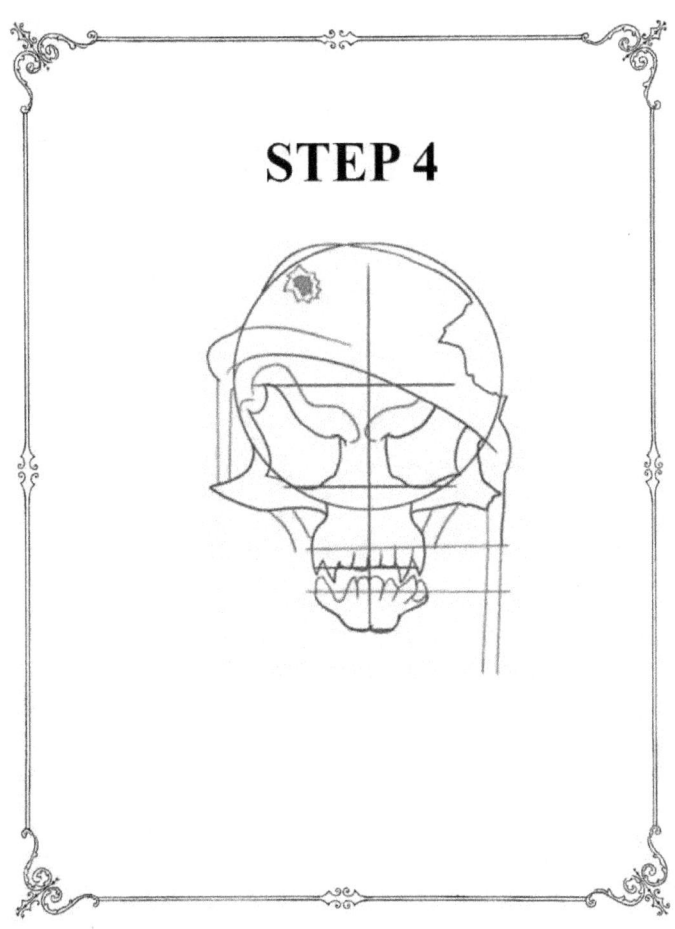

STEP 5

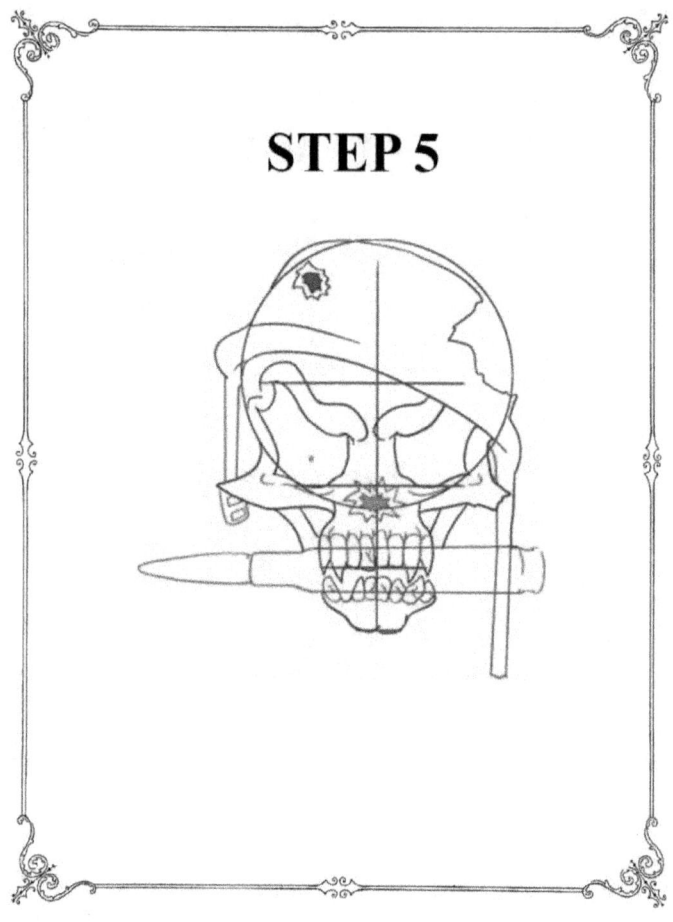

STEP 6

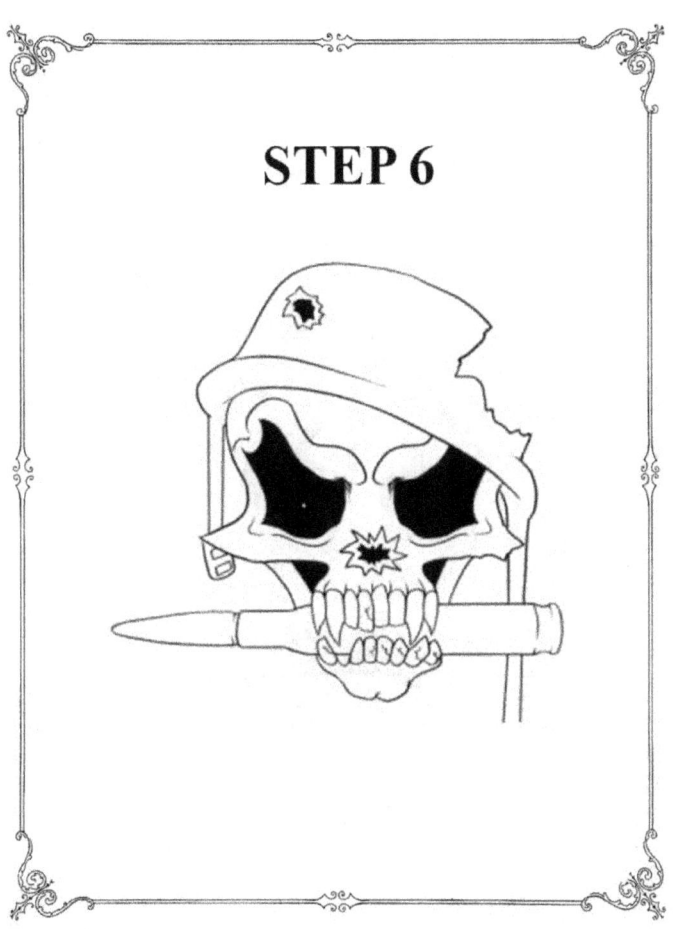

SPADE SKULL

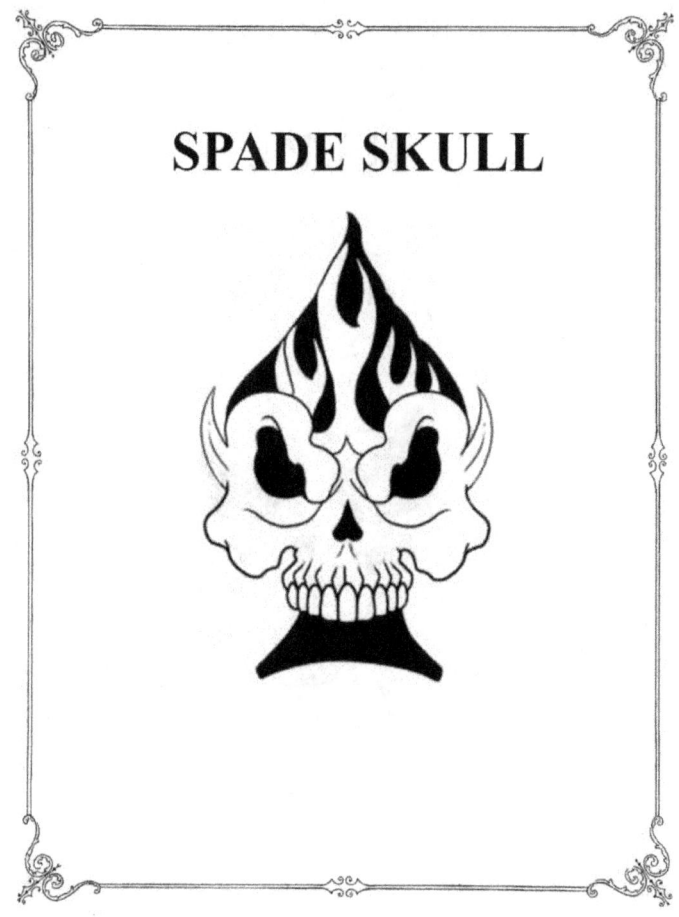

STEP 1

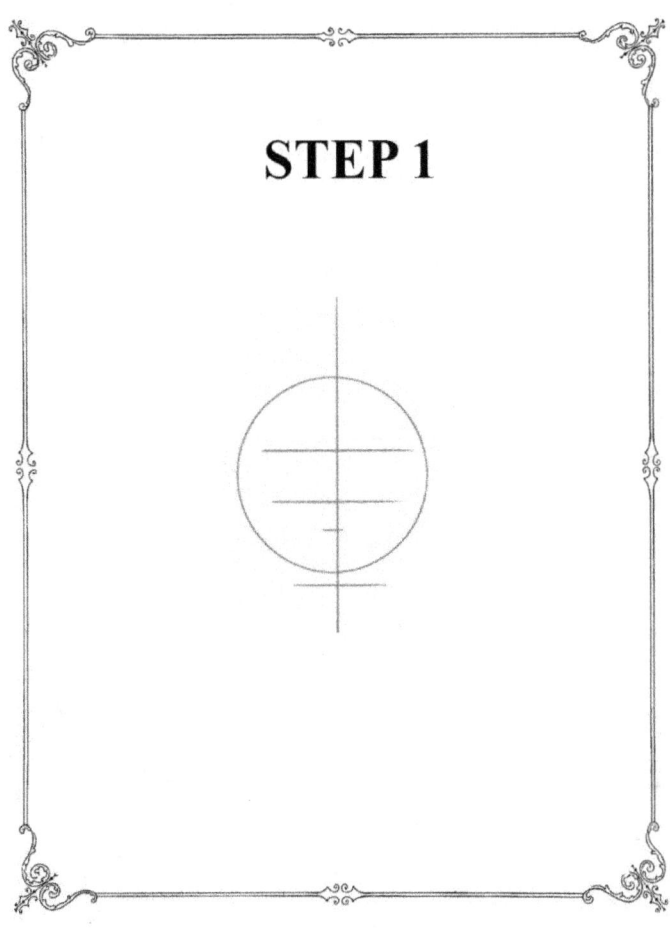

STEP 2

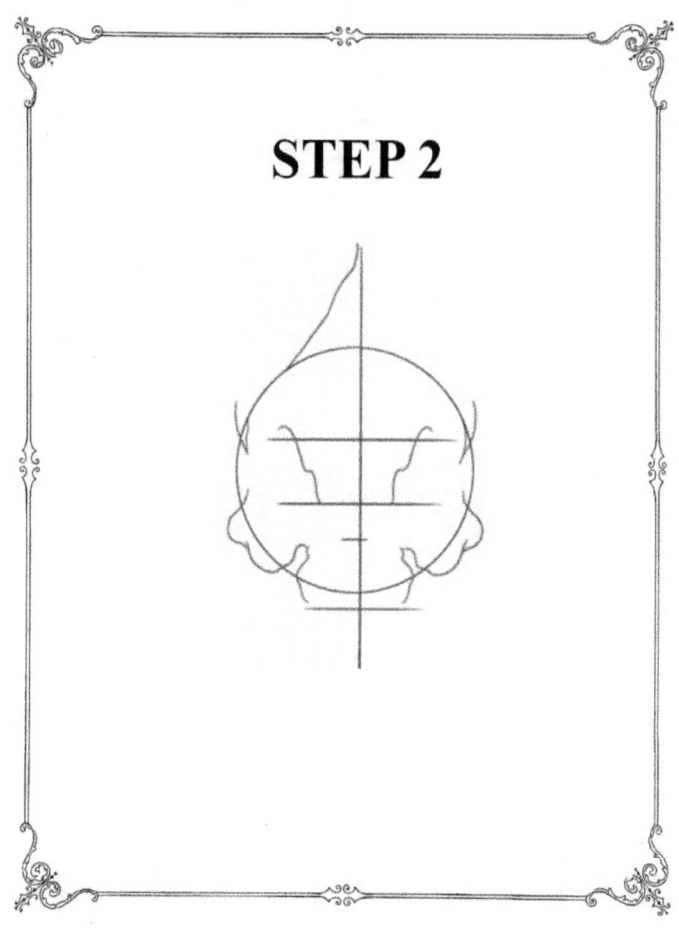

STEP 3

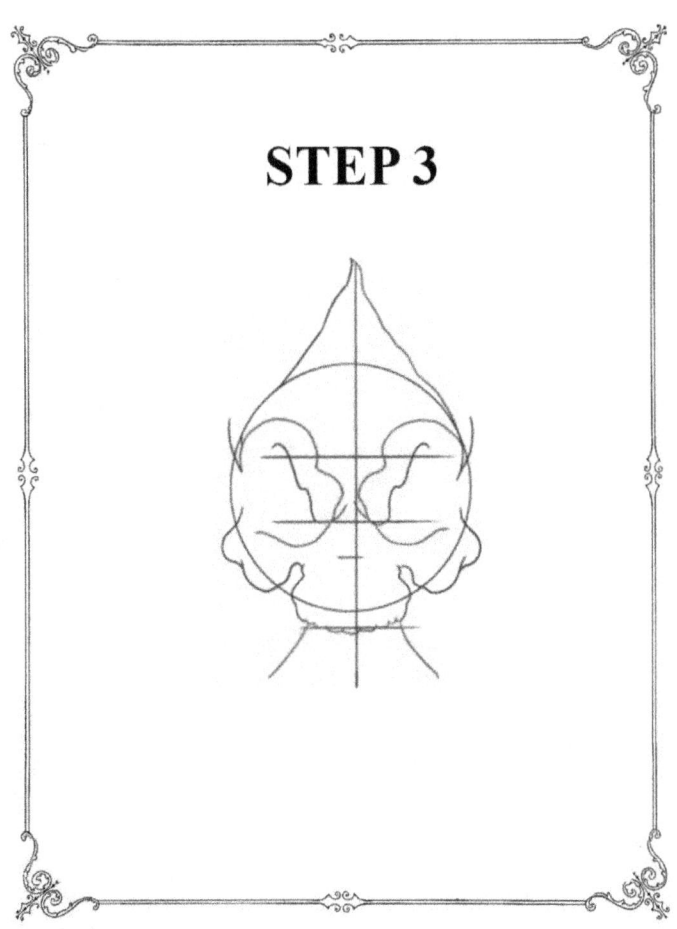

STEP 4

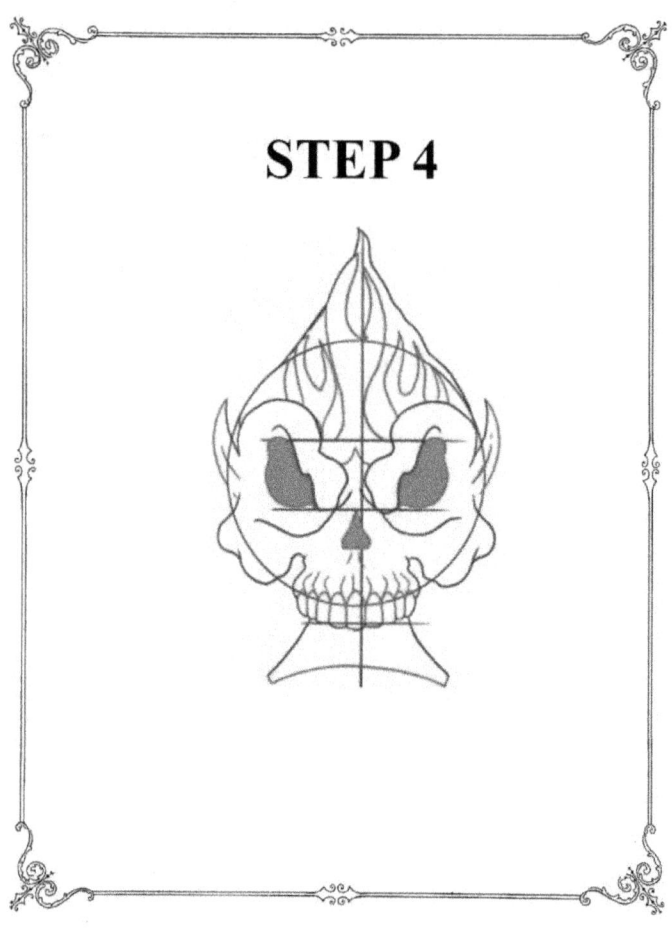

STEP 5

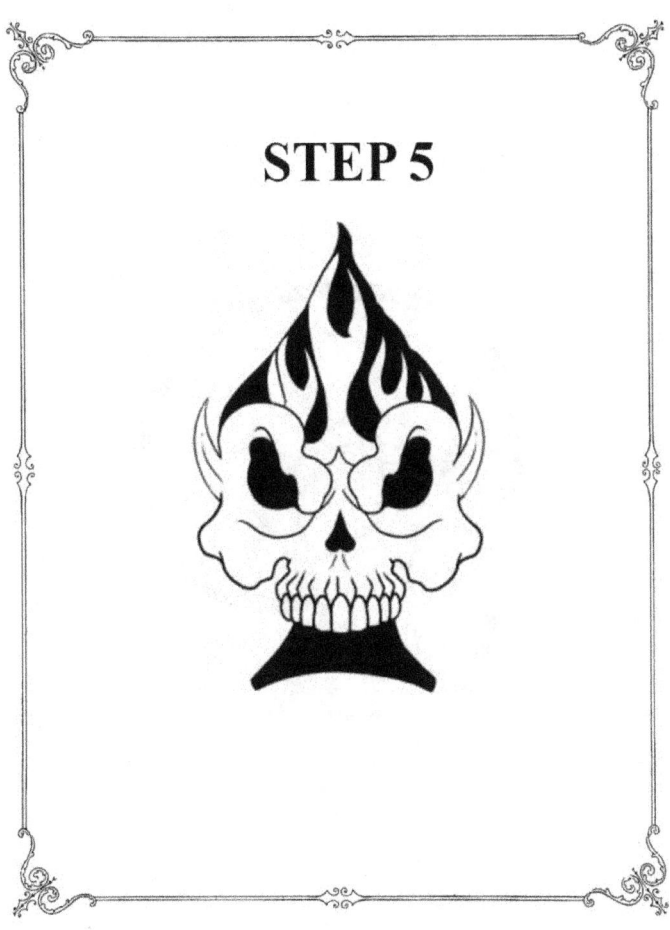

SUGAR SKULL

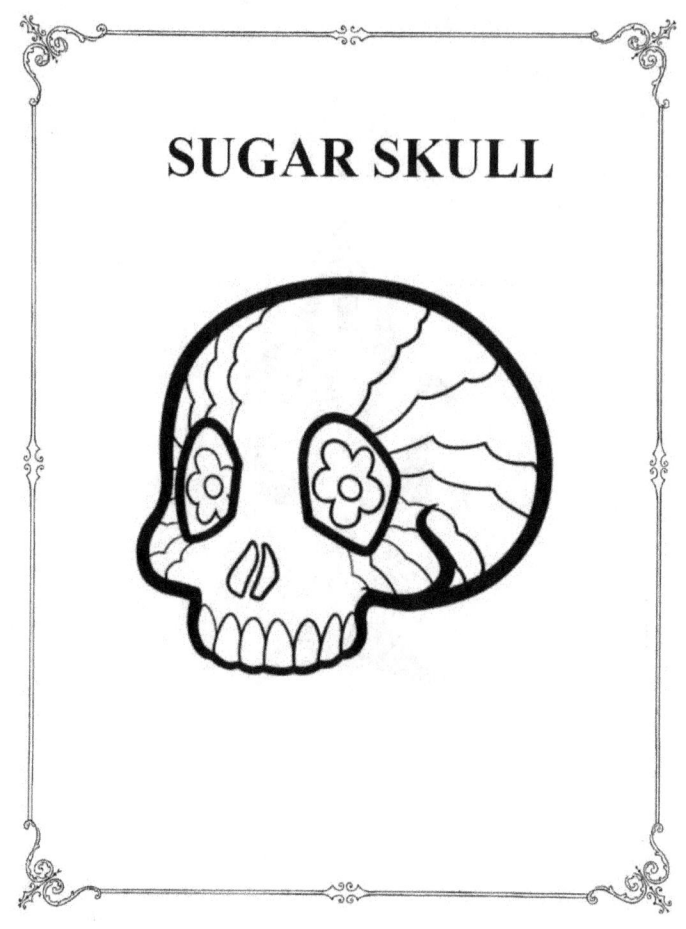

STEP 1

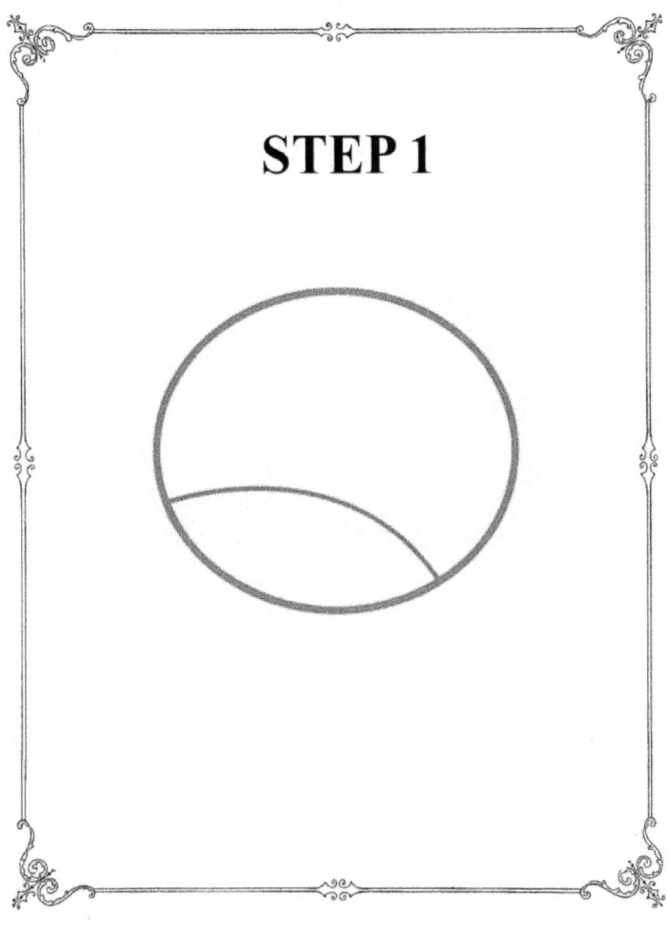

STEP 2

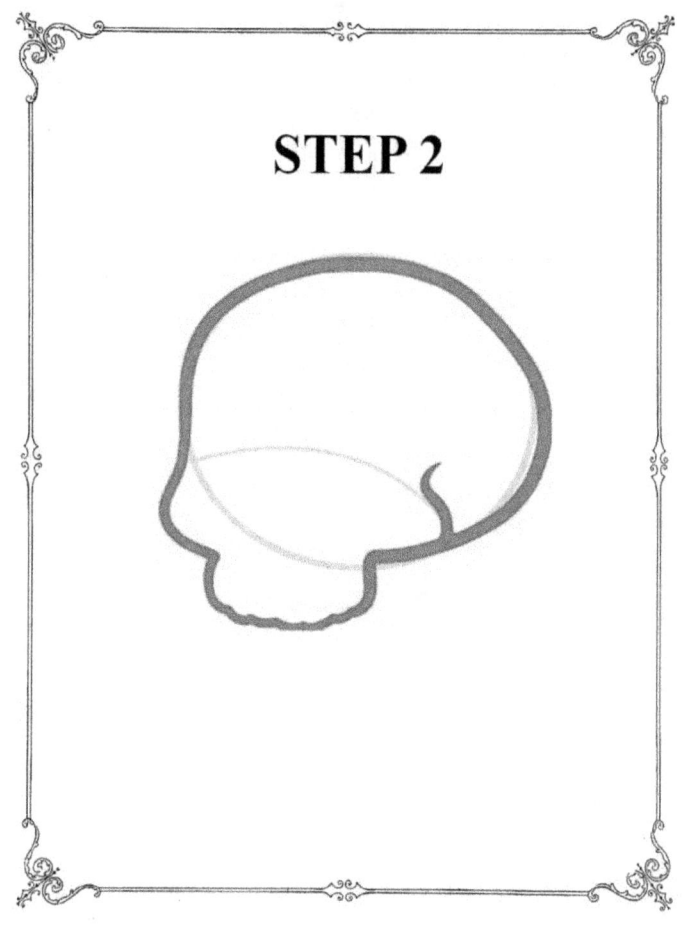

STEP 3

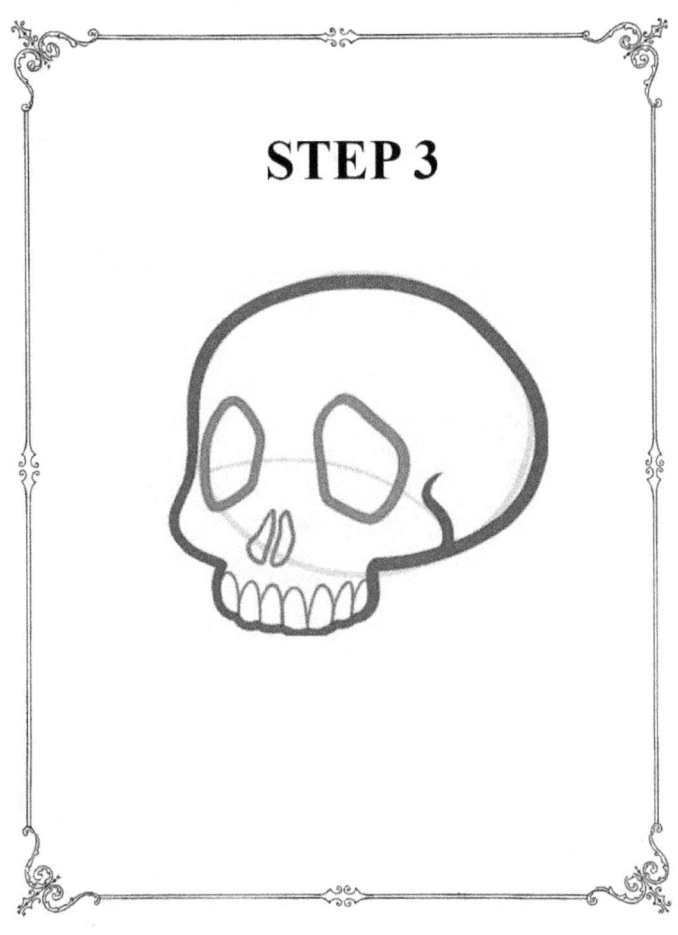

STEP 4

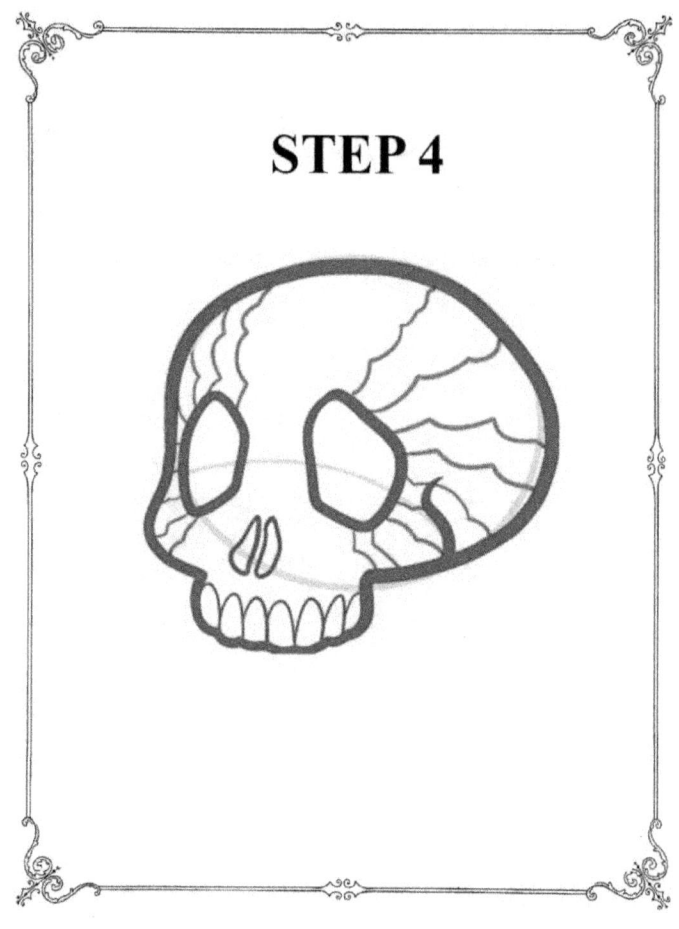

STEP 5

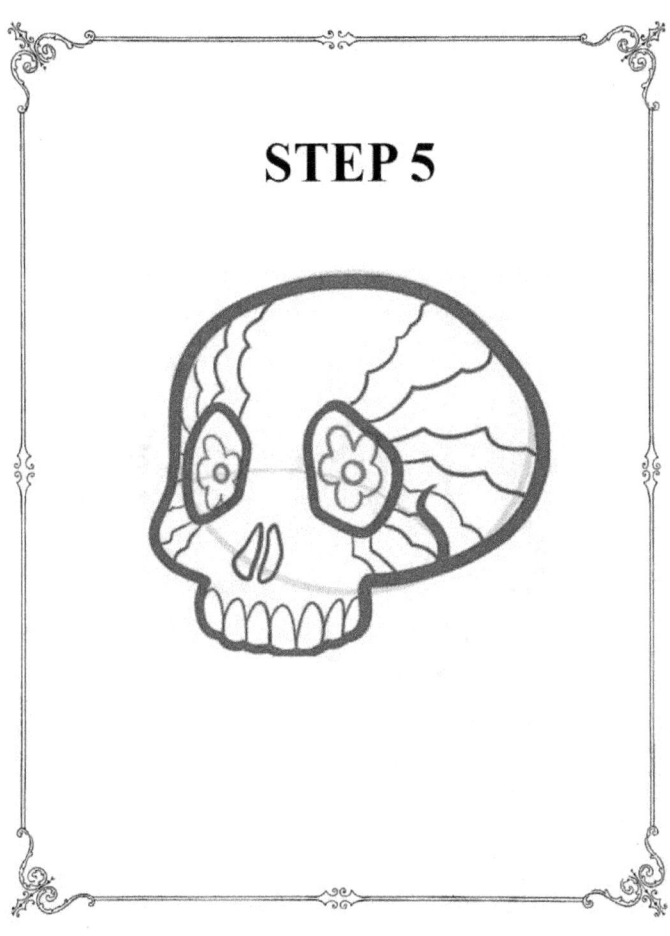

STEP 6

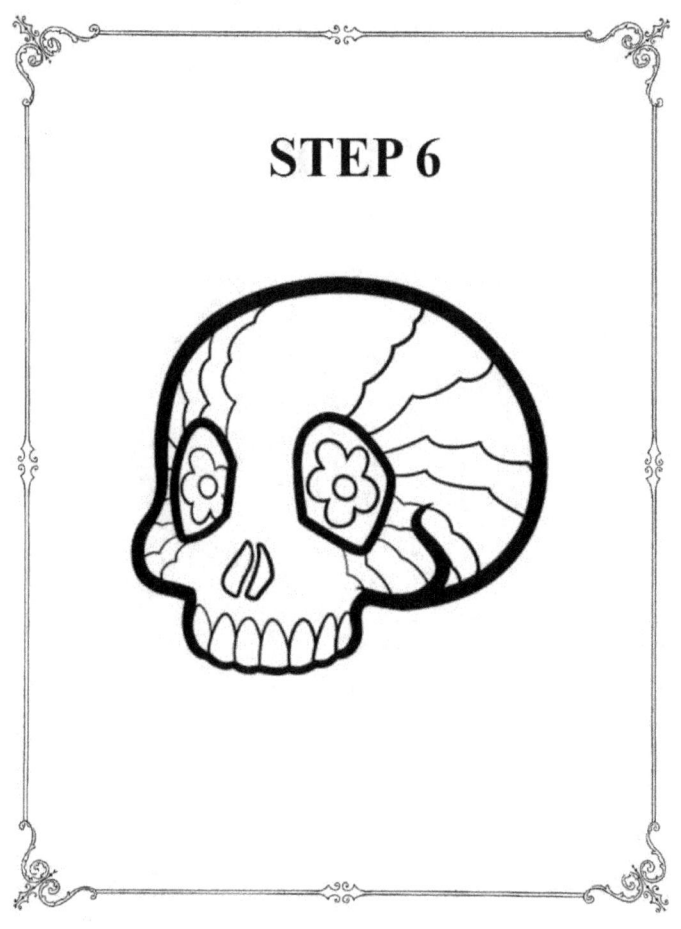